MAKING SHAPES

Editor:
Jon Richards

Design:

David West • CHILDREN'S BOOKS
Designer: David Millea

Illustrator:
Tony Kenyon

Photography:
Roger Vlitos
Models:
David Millea

*The publishers wish to point out that all the
photographs reproduced in this book have either been posed
by models or obtained from photographic agencies.*

© Aladdin Books Ltd 1995
Created and produced by
NW Books
28 Percy Street
London W1P OLD

First published in Great Britain in 1995 by
Watts Books
96 Leonard Street
London EC2A 4RH
ISBN 0 7496 2113 3
All rights reserved
Printed in Belgium

SCIENCE FOR FUN

MAKING SHAPES

GARY GIBSON

WATTS BOOKS
London • Sydney

CONTENTS

INTRODUCTION

You may have walked across a bridge and wondered how it is able to support your weight, and the weight of bicycles, cars and trucks. Objects around us assume a variety of shapes and sizes, depending on the job that they must do. How does the shape of an egg make it strong? How are stalactites formed? How does a spring keep its shape, and how can plastic lose its shape? This book contains a selection of exciting "hands-on" projects to help answer some of these fascinating questions.

When this symbol appears, adult supervision is required.

GET AN ADULT TO HELP YOU WITH THIS

MYSTERIOUS SHAPES

We can learn a lot about materials and their shapes from nature. But all of these shapes are solids, and have at least two sides. What about a one-sided shape? What special properties does it have?

MAKE A MÖBIUS STRIP

1 Colour both sides of three paper strips. Tape together the first strip to make a band.

2 Repeat with the second strip, but twist the strip once before sticking the ends together.

WHY IT WORKS

The first strip will make two new bands, the second a single long band and the third, two linked bands. This is a trick of mathematics. The second and third strips are calles Möbius strips, after their inventor.

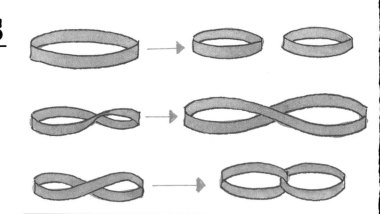

3 Twist the third strip twice before taping the ends together.

4 Finally, cut each band in half, along their length.

FURTHER IDEAS

Draw a pencil line along each of the bands. You will find that the line continues along both "sides" of the second band!

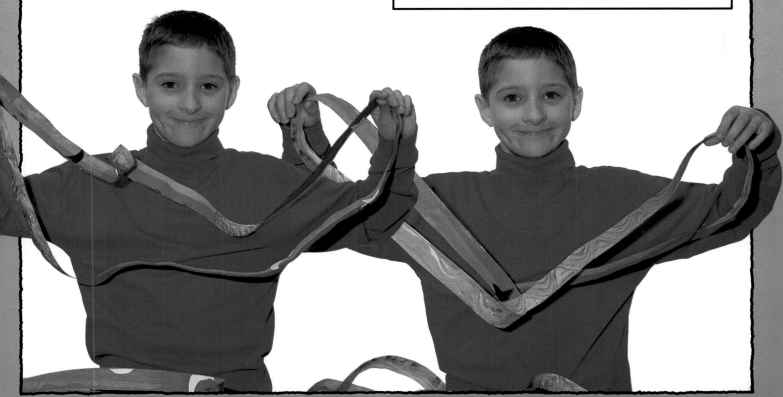

SHAPES IN NATURE

You can find crystals everywhere around you. Gemstones, like emeralds, have always fascinated people. Salt, sand and sugar are also made from crystals. Then there are the quartz crystals in your watch and the silicon in your computer.

GROW SOME CRYSTALS

1 Pour water from the hot water tap into a clean glass jar. Stir in one spoonful of potash of alum at a time.

2 Keep adding alum until no more will dissolve. You now have a saturated solution. Leave it for two days.

3 Drain the saturated solution through a sieve. Save the water for later and keep the crystals.

WHY IT WORKS

When the alum dissolved, the particles it was made up of spread out in the water. As the water evaporated, there was not enough water to dissolve all of the alum. The particles of alum were forced back together again to make crystals.

4 Look at the crystals with a magnifying glass. They are different sizes. Are they the same shape?

FURTHER IDEAS
Pour the spare saturated solution into a jar. Hang a crystal from a pencil and hang it in the jar. See it grow over a few days.

HANGING ROCKS

Rainwater can dissolve some types of solid rock. Sometimes the water drips into a cave underground and, as it does so, it leaves the solid behind. Over time this solid slowly builds up to form columns which hang from the roof, called stalactites.

GROW A STALACTITE

1 Make a saturated solution with Epsom salts in a jar of hot water.

2 Fill two glasses with the saturated solution.

3 Fix paper clips to the ends of some wool. Hang the ends in the two glasses.

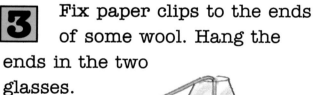

4 Place a saucer under the wool. Leave in a warm, undisturbed place for a week.

5 Watch as the stalactite grows down from the wool to the saucer over a number of days.

WHY IT WORKS

The saturated solution soaks into the wool and spreads along its length. Some of it drips off the wool and onto the saucer. As it drips, the water evaporates, leaving behind a column of salts.

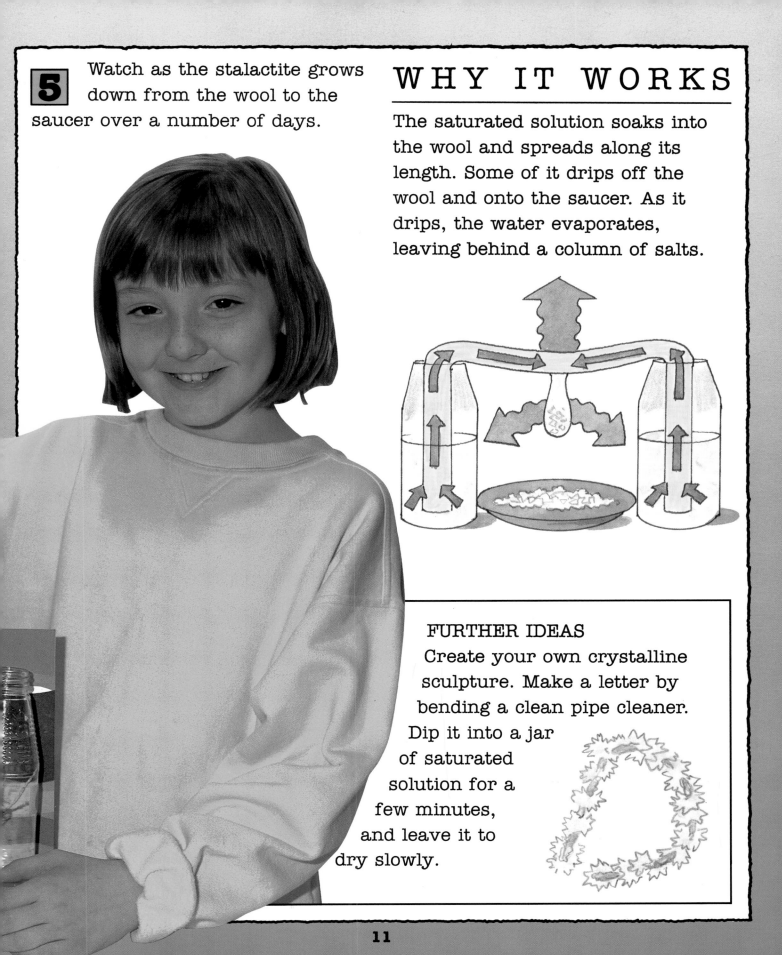

FURTHER IDEAS
Create your own crystalline sculpture. Make a letter by bending a clean pipe cleaner. Dip it into a jar of saturated solution for a few minutes, and leave it to dry slowly.

SHAPE AND STRENGTH

Everybody knows how easy it is to break an egg. The eggshell is thin and can break with the slightest knock. However, an egg can also be very strong. It must survive the impact of falling to the ground when the egg is laid. Nature has produced the shape to be light and strong.

TEST THE STRENGTH OF AN EGG

1 Find a large tray. Stand up the egg at one side of the tray using plasticine to hold it in place.

2 At the other side of the tray make two piles of coins exactly the same height as the egg. The egg and two piles should make a triangle.

3 Wrap some books in plastic wrap for protection. Support one book on the coins and egg.

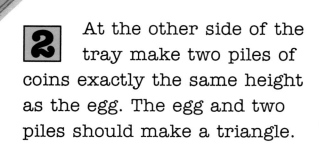

4 Add another book. Watch the egg carefully as you add each book. How many books can the egg help support before it breaks?

WHY IT WORKS

The shape of the egg makes it both hollow and light. It has an arch at each end, a good structure for supporting weight. The egg has a lot of strength lengthways because the tall arches spread more weight. It is much easier to break when on its side because these arches are weaker.

FURTHER IDEAS
This time compare the egg's strength to that of some paper shapes, such as a box, a pyramid and a tube.

HANGING AROUND

One of the most important properties of any material is its strength. A material that snaps under the slightest load is not much use. Nature has made some of the strongest materials around. For example, the silken strands in a spider's web are stronger than steel of the same thickness.

FIND THE STRONGEST STRIP

1 Cut three strips of paper, tissue paper, and plastic from a plastic bag, making them the same length and width.

2 Using tape, fasten some wooden dowel to each end of the strips.

GET AN ADULT TO DO THIS FOR YOU

3 Ask an adult to cut two small holes on each side of the top of three paper cups to make three baskets.

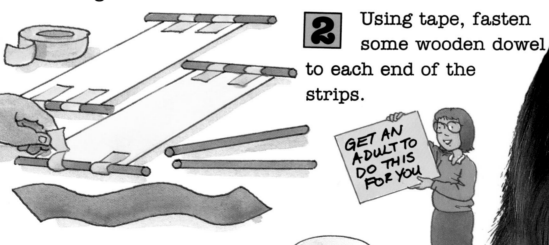

4 Attach a basket to one of the wooden dowels. Tie string around the other wooden dowel.

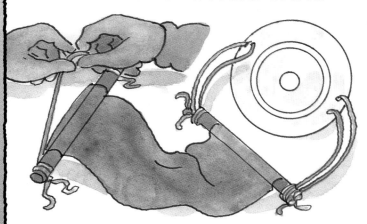

5 Hang each strip from a wall. Slowly add weights to the baskets until each strip breaks.

WHY IT WORKS

Plastic is the strongest because its particles are held together by very strong bonds. Paper is made from densely packed fibres that can be split apart quite easily. Tissue paper fibres are not so densely packed, making it the weakest of the three.

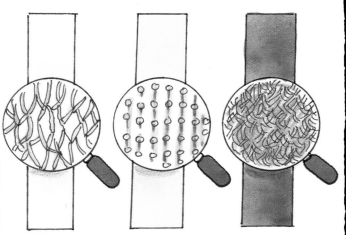

FURTHER IDEAS

Repeat the test with plastic strips of different widths. How does this affect the strength?

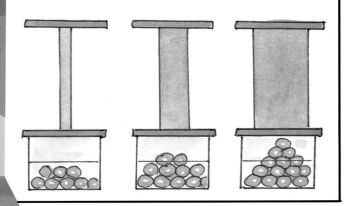

MAKING MATERIALS

The materials we find in nature are called "raw" materials. We use many of these, and change them to make other products. Glass is made from sand and paper is made from wood. We can improve a material by changing its properties.

MAKE A PAPIER-MÂCHÉ BOWL

1 Mix some flour and water in a large plastic bowl, keeping the mixture runny.

2 Tear up strips of newspaper, and soak them in the mixture.

3 Inflate a balloon. Starting near the balloon's middle, apply the soaked paper in layers.

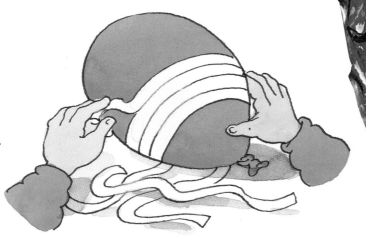

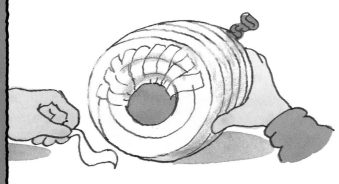

4 To make the bowl's base, sit the balloon on a plastic lid. Cover the lid with more papier-mâché.

5 Leave overnight, then remove the balloon. Paint the finished bowl for decoration. Varnish it for extra protection.

WHY IT WORKS

Paper is made up of many thousands of tiny strands of wood fibres. The mixture of flour and water fills the gaps between these fibres. As the mixture dries, it sets hard, making the paper rigid. It keeps its new shape unless soaked again in water.

FURTHER IDEAS

You can use a real bowl as a mould. Cover the bowl with plastic wrap first to make the papier-mâché easy to remove.

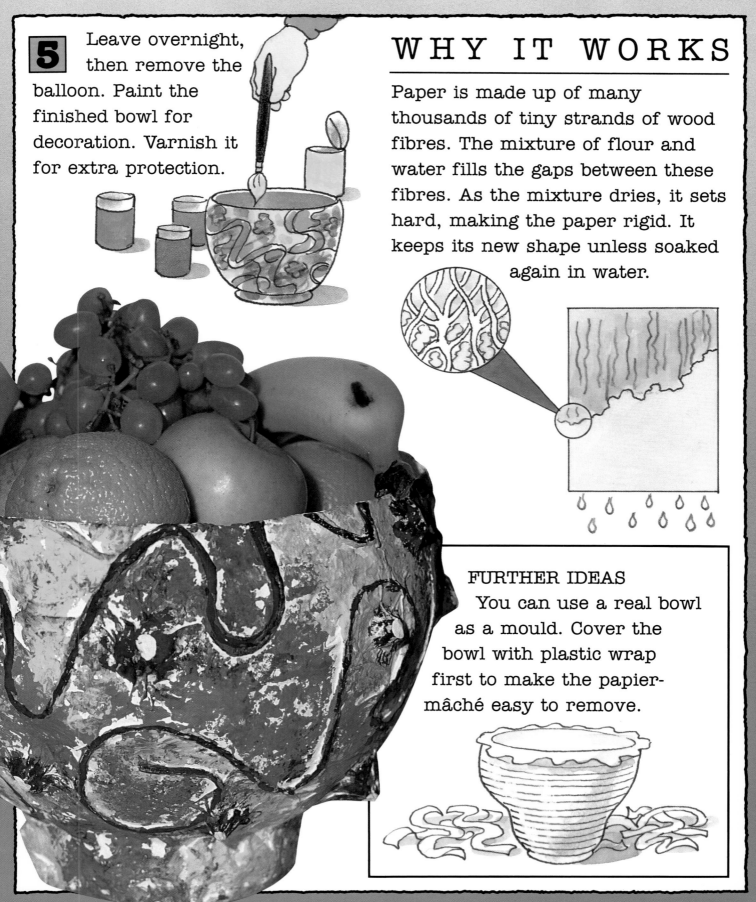

FILLING SHAPES

Like papier-mâché, materials such as cement, plaster and gypsum alter their form when mixed with water and allowed to dry. Unlike papier-mâché, these substances can be poured into moulds, and used to form shapes, from small statues to enormous buildings.

PLASTER OF PARIS

1 Find a clean rubber glove. Lubricate the inside with a few drops of washing up liquid.

2 Hang the glove upside down with a couple of pegs to hold it open.

3 Use a wooden stick to mix some plaster of Paris with cold water in a glass jar. Mix thoroughly until creamy.

4 Pour the mixture into the glove. Make sure it is filled to the top.

5 Leave overnight to dry out. Gently peel off the glove from the plaster underneath. Be careful because the plaster is quite brittle.

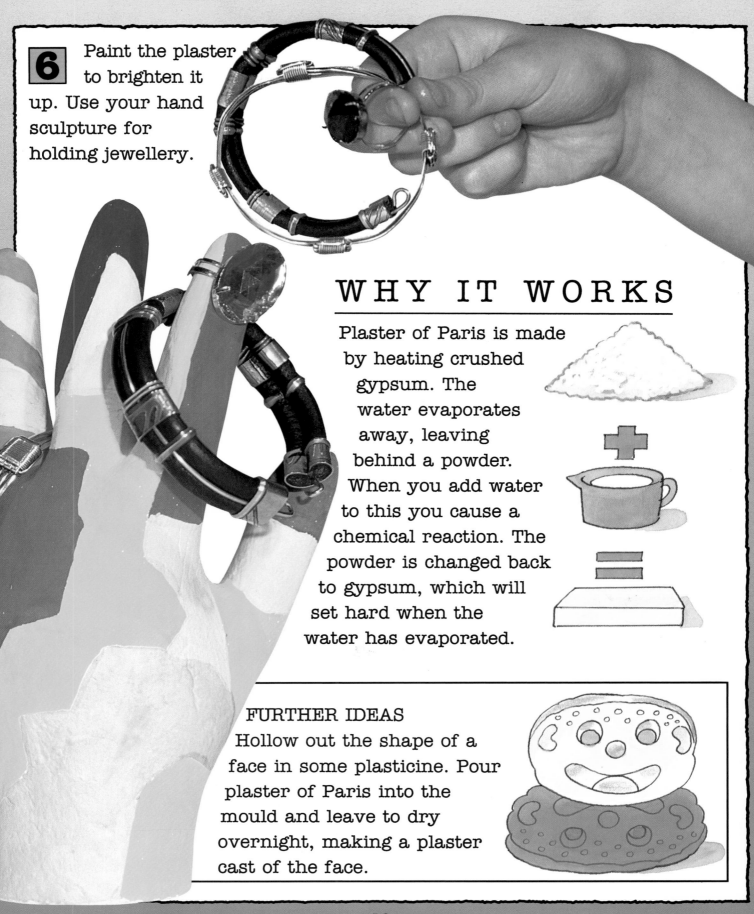

6 Paint the plaster to brighten it up. Use your hand sculpture for holding jewellery.

WHY IT WORKS

Plaster of Paris is made by heating crushed gypsum. The water evaporates away, leaving behind a powder. When you add water to this you cause a chemical reaction. The powder is changed back to gypsum, which will set hard when the water has evaporated.

FURTHER IDEAS
Hollow out the shape of a face in some plasticine. Pour plaster of Paris into the mould and leave to dry overnight, making a plaster cast of the face.

ELASTIC MATERIALS

Not only elastic bands are elastic. Most things have some springiness, especially in certain shapes. One of the reasons metals are so useful is because of their springiness or elasticity. This means that as you pull the material out of shape it tries to return to that shape.

MAKE A JACK IN THE BOX

1 Ask an adult to coil a length of stiff wire around a broom handle to make a spring.

2 Cut the neck from a plastic drink bottle. Fix the spring to the bottom with tape.

3 Ask an adult to secure a lid with paper fasteners.

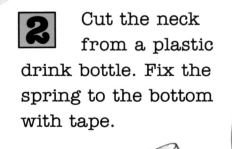

GET AN ADULT TO DO THIS FOR YOU

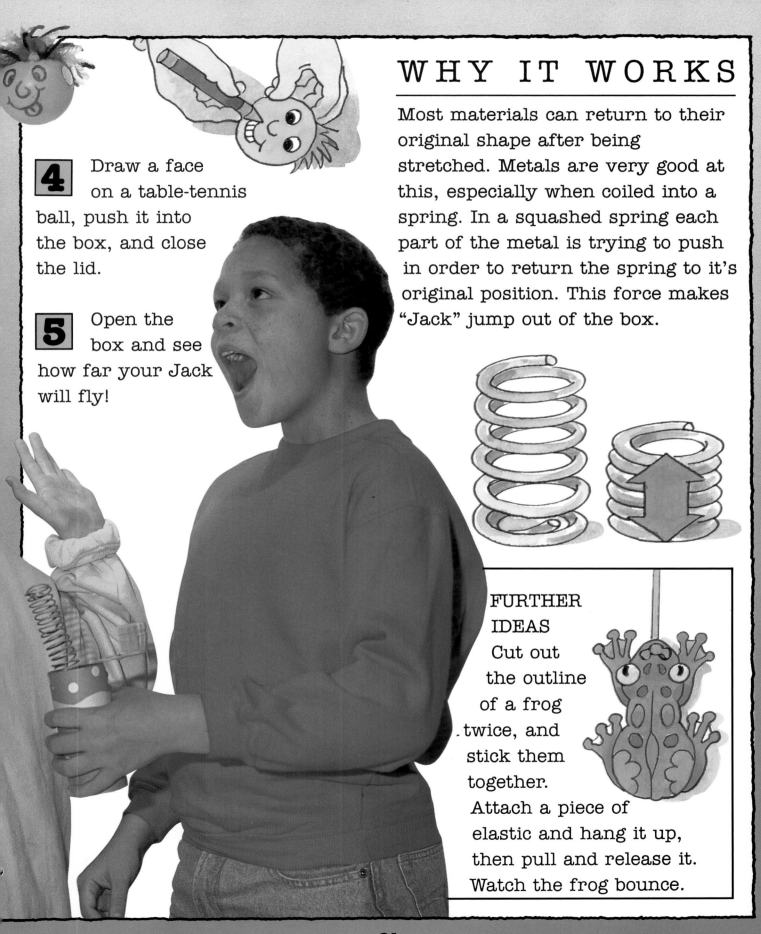

4 Draw a face on a table-tennis ball, push it into the box, and close the lid.

5 Open the box and see how far your Jack will fly!

WHY IT WORKS

Most materials can return to their original shape after being stretched. Metals are very good at this, especially when coiled into a spring. In a squashed spring each part of the metal is trying to push in order to return the spring to it's original position. This force makes "Jack" jump out of the box.

FURTHER IDEAS Cut out the outline of a frog twice, and stick them together. Attach a piece of elastic and hang it up, then pull and release it. Watch the frog bounce.

SHAPELESS PLASTICS

Some materials can be pulled into new shapes which they then keep. They do not go back to their previous shape as an elastic material would. Such materials are called "plastic". For example wet clay is plastic because you can mould it into any shape you want and it stays that way.

MAKE SOME PLASTIC MILK

1 Ask an adult to slowly warm some creamy milk in a pan.

2 When the milk is just starting to bubble, slowly stir in a little vinegar.

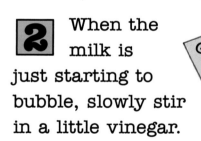

GET AN ADULT TO HELP YOU WITH THESE

3 Keep stirring. Within seconds the mixture should go rubbery.

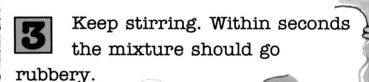

4 Let this rubbery mixture cool. Wash it under the cold water tap, and examine the "plastic".

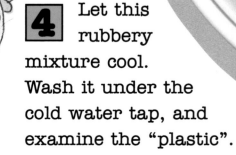

WHY IT WORKS

Vinegar is a member of the chemical family called acids. When it is added to the warm milk, it sets up a chemical reaction which rearranges the particles in the milk. Instead of being "runny" and free to move, they clump together. It is this clump that becomes the lump of "plastic".

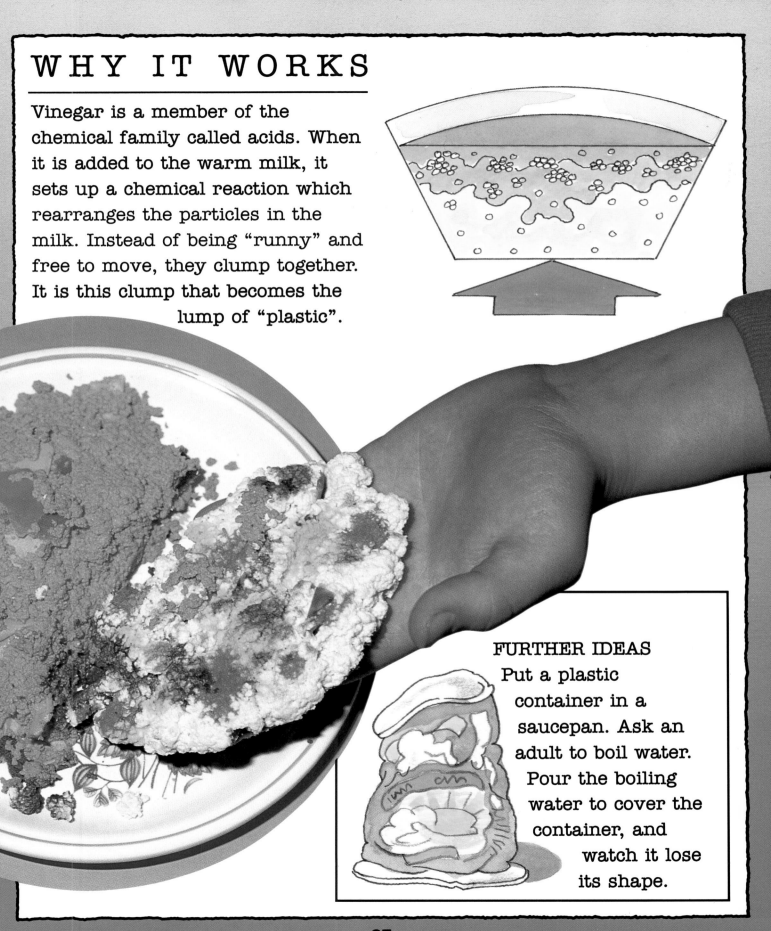

FURTHER IDEAS
Put a plastic container in a saucepan. Ask an adult to boil water. Pour the boiling water to cover the container, and watch it lose its shape.

FIBRES AND THREADS

Fibres are long, thin, flexible strands of material like threads. Each of your hairs is a fibre. Natural fibres also include animal fur and wool from sheep. Fibres can be twisted together to make yarn, which can be woven in turn to make fabrics or cloth.

MAKE A LOOM

1 Cut out an odd number of notches along the top and bottom of some card.

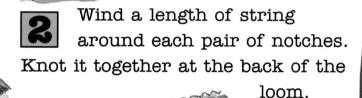

GET AN ADULT TO DO THIS FOR YOU

2 Wind a length of string around each pair of notches. Knot it together at the back of the loom.

3 Weave some thick wool across the loom, in and out of the string. To change colour, tie another strip to the old one.

4 When you have filled the loom, tie off the last strip of fabric. Lift the weaving off the card.

5 Push lengths of a dowel through the top and bottom warp threads. Hang it up as a decoration.

WHY IT WORKS

The strings going up and down are called the warp threads. The threads going across are called the weft threads. By weaving the threads together the finished fabric is strong. The closer the weave, the stronger the finished fabric.

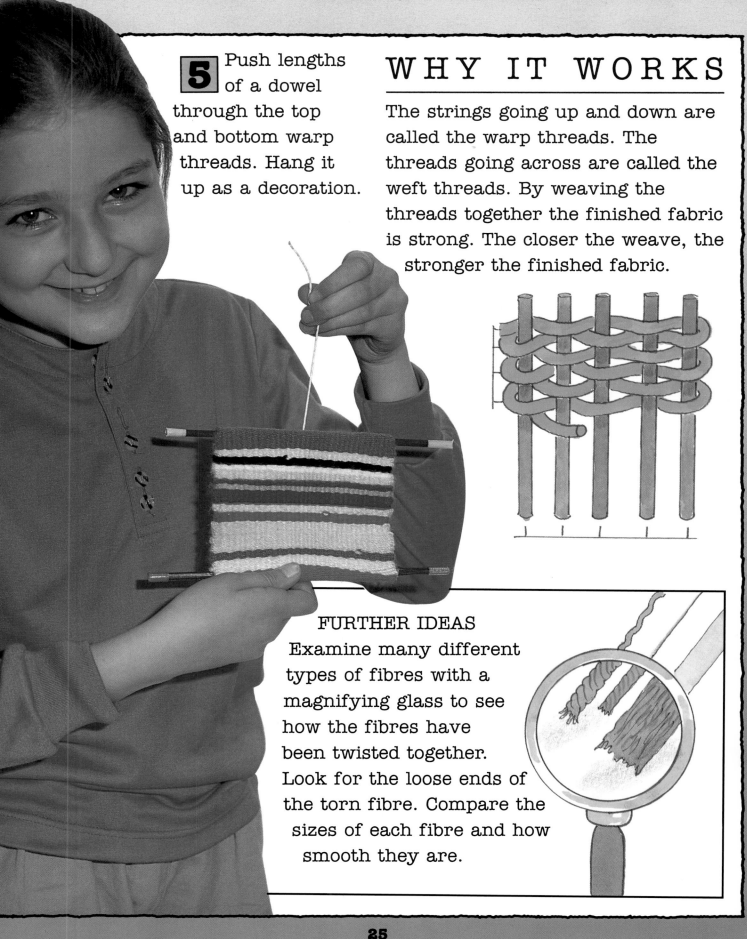

FURTHER IDEAS

Examine many different types of fibres with a magnifying glass to see how the fibres have been twisted together. Look for the loose ends of the torn fibre. Compare the sizes of each fibre and how smooth they are.

FITTING IT TOGETHER

Some shapes fit neatly together to cover an area without overlapping or leaving spaces. This is called "tessellation". Examples are the bricks in a wall and the squares on a chessboard. An example in nature is the honeycomb in a beehive, where hexagonal cells fit snugly together.

MAKE A TRIANGLE PUZZLE

1 On a large sheet of white card, draw a triangle with sides 30 cm long using a ruler.

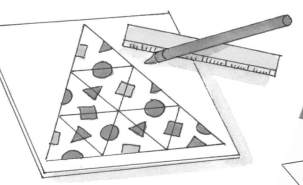

2 Divide the large triangle into nine smaller ones. Each side should be 10 cm long.

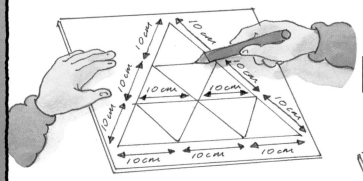

3 On each of the triangles draw a circle, a square and a triangle as shown.

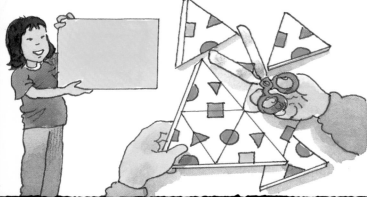

4 Use sharp scissors to carefully cut out each of the nine small triangles.

WHY IT WORKS

A tessellated structure, like a beehive, must have no gaps or overlapping shapes. Only certain shapes, such as triangles and hexagons, will tessellate. To cover a surface with circles, which do not tessellate, you would have to overlap the shapes, or leave gaps.

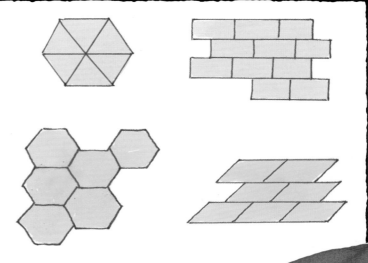

5 Challenge a friend with your triangle puzzle. They should be able to match up the pattern to correctly put together the big triangle again.

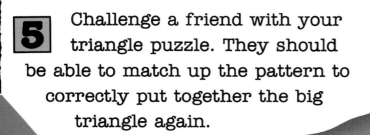

FURTHER IDEAS

A mosaic is like a tessellation, but the shapes that fit together are not the same. Cut out lots of small card shapes. Glue them down to fit the outline of a drawing on card. Make the gaps as small as possible.

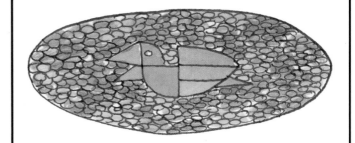

BRIDGES

Since earliest times people have built bridges to cross rivers and other obstacles. The first bridges were probably tree trunks laid across a stream. Later bridges were built from arches to carry heavier loads. Modern bridges use either steel girders or suspension cables.

BUILD MODEL BRIDGES

1 Find six blocks of wood to make three bridges. Tape pencils to two of the corners.

2 Ask an adult to cut some strips of thick card the same width as the blocks.

GET AN ADULT TO HELP YOU WITH THIS

3 Place a strip of card between two blocks to make a beam bridge. On the second, support this strip with an arch.

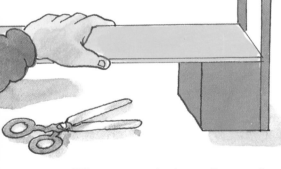

4 On the third, tie string to the pencils, and tape the string to the strip to make a suspension bridge.

5 Draw a river on a sheet of card. Place it under your bridges.

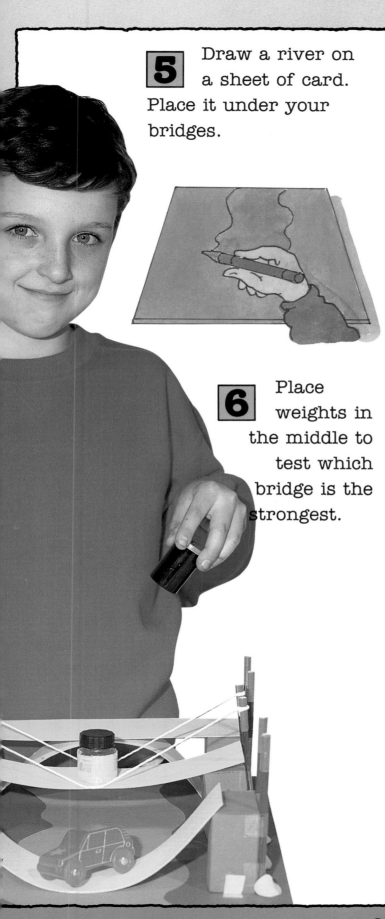

6 Place weights in the middle to test which bridge is the strongest.

WHY IT WORKS

The beam bridge is the weakest because the weight is not spread. The string in the suspension bridge takes some of the weight. The arch is strongest because the weight is spread out over its whole length.

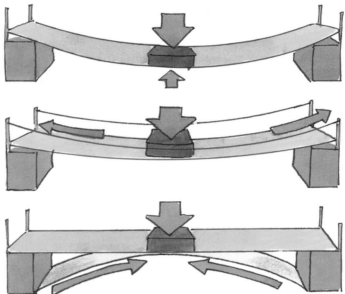

FURTHER IDEAS

Try making a bridge frame out of plastic drinking straws. Join the straws together by pushing the end of one into another.

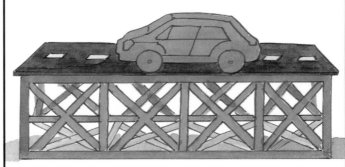

FANTASTIC SHAPE FACTS

The longest stalactite in the world is 59 m (195 ft) long and can be found in the Cueva de Nerja in Spain. The tallest stalagmite is only 32 m (105 ft) high and is in the Krásnohorká Cave in Slovakia.

Diamonds are amongst the most valuable objects. The largest was discovered in South Africa in 1905. The Cullinan diamond, as it was called, was subsequently cut into 106 separate, polished stones.

The largest bird, the ostrich, also lays the largest egg. Ostrich eggs are usually 20 cm long and can support a person weighing 127 kg. In contrast, the egg of a hummingbird is only 1 cm long and weighs under half a gram!

The longest cable suspension bridge can be found crossing the Humber estuary in England. It is 1,410 m (4,626 ft) long and its two towers stretch 162 m (533 ft) above the water. It is so long that builders had to take into account the curvature of the Earth when the bridge was under construction.

Contrary to public opinion the Earth is not round. It is, in fact, shaped like a slightly squashed ball. The distance around the equator is longer than the distance around the North and South Poles. The technical name for such a shape is an oblate spheroid.

Over millions of years, fish and other creatures that swim have developed a body shape which allows them to cut through the water with the minimum of effort. Humans have learnt from nature's design and have copied these streamlined shapes for boats and submarines to make them travel faster through the water.

Airplanes can fly because of the shape of their wings. These are made so that air flowing over the top of the wing travels faster than the air flowing below the wing. The result is that the wing and the plane are pushed upwards into the air. The wings of birds, bats and insects also use this principle to stay aloft.

GLOSSARY

Arch

A shape, roughly semi-circular, that is capable of supporting a great deal of weight.

Brittle

When an object can be easily broken.

Crystal

A solid body where the atoms are arranged in a rigid structure.

Elastic

An elastic object will recover its original shape after being moulded.

Möbius strip

A surface that has only one side. It is made by joining the two ends of a strip that has been twisted around once.

Particle

A tiny piece of a substance.

Plastic

When a body can be shaped into another form, it is said to be plastic. Its properties allow it to be moulded and then retain its new shape.

Rigid

When an object is stiff and inflexible, it is said to be rigid. Its structure will not allow it to be bent or shaped into any other shape.

Saturated

When a substance has been filled to its fullest possible extent.

Streamlined

The quality of a shape which allows it to travel through either air or water with minimum effort. It achieves this by not creating drag, which may slow a body down.

Structure

The arrangement of parts to form an entire object.

Tessellation

The ability of shapes to fit together neatly and cover an area without overlapping or leaving any spaces.

Weaving

To form a fabric by interlacing fibres. Horizontal threads are woven through vertical threads, to create the finished cloth.

INDEX